Terms and Conditions

LEGAL NOTICE

The Publisher has strived to be as accurate and complete as possible in the creation of this report, notwithstanding the fact that he does not warrant or represent at any time that the contents within are accurate due to the rapidly changing nature of the Internet.

While all attempts have been made to verify information provided in this publication, the Publisher assumes no responsibility for errors, omissions, or contrary interpretation of the subject matter herein. Any perceived slights of specific persons, peoples, or organizations are unintentional.

In practical advice books, like anything else in life, there are no guarantees of income made. Readers are cautioned to reply on their own judgment about their individual circumstances to act accordingly.

This book is not intended for use as a source of legal, business, accounting or financial advice. All readers are advised to seek services of competent professionals in legal, business, accounting and finance fields.

You are encouraged to print this book for easy reading.

Table Of Contents

Foreword

Chapter 1:
Network Marketing Twitter Basics

Chapter 2:
Know The Difference Between Posting And Spamming

Chapter 3:
Be Clear On What You Are Promoting

Chapter 4:
Plan How To Communicate With Others To Convey Professionalism

Chapter 5:
Learn How To Participate With The Community

Chapter 6:
Learn How To Make The Most Of Your Account And Profile

Chapter 7:
Avoid Over Promoting

Chapter 8:
Follow And Use Relevant Tweets

Wrapping Up

Foreword

Making a success of any business today would be better served if the internet was used. The internet being the far reaching tool that it is, helps to create the desired revenue for the successful business venture. The internet, specifically the social media tools have over time proven to be the most successful. Learn about Twitter here.

Top Twitter Techniques
How To Tweet your Way To Network Marketing Success

Chapter 1:
Network Marketing Twitter Basics

Synopsis

Tools like twitter can effective create the attention that is necessary in getting the information about the business to the wider audience. This is done with virtually no cost involved.

The planned site must is attractive enough to be the cause of the twitter exercise thus ensuring the desired amount of traffic to the site. Providing material that is worth discussion or viewing with the intention of dispersing information is very important as this is what will cause the interest to stay.

The Basics

As the twitter platform is comparatively personal. Ensuring the exchanges have some form of follow ups is beneficial to the host. If the users are made to feel special, then it is almost guaranteed that the host site will garner the desired traffic which will eventually be converted to revenue.

Spending some time to personally address issues or comments will encourage the user to stay loyal as they perceive their participation to be well received and valued.

Being consistent, as in a daily basis also is another element to consider at it allows feedback and comments to be shared from a more current standpoint.

Building a rapport with the users is always a good idea as both parties will eventually attest to benefit from the exchanges. Building the list of customers, prospects, potential buyers all depends on whether the material being discussed is of high interest value.

Having a great product or service is of no value if it is not made known to the masses.

Chapter 2:
Know The Difference Between Posting And Spamming

Synopsis

Spamming is perhaps the most annoying application that most internet users are weary of. Basically the spam element involved the sending of material in a continuous and abundant manner causing the recipient to be overwhelmed with unwanted material.

This will basically cause a lot of problems when the inbox becomes jammed with all the unwanted solicitations.

Therefore one needs to be careful to ensure the material posted is designed and posted in a way to does not cause it to fall into the spam category.

The Differences

Most spasms target individual users who use the direct email messaging platform regularly. These email listing are more often than not "stolen" from other more legitimate sources with the intention of using the said list to post the material categorized as spam.

The two main types of spam but both are an equally unwelcomed solicitation.

Postings however are very different in its original design and intention aspect. Though having the same desired reach of the target audience, the posting element is used to create visibility on the internet but with the distinct difference of wanting to create an interaction.

The message is replied to in the form of email, internet forums and use net. The benefits of posting may include being able to harness direct visitors to the site, branding position, promotion of the site and its material of services or products, creating external links and many more positive contributions.

Posting also provides maximum visibility online. The classified ad site can be used without being feared as being categorized as spam and with this comes the advantage of being marketed effectively.

The hopeful result here is that through the posting even the uninterested viewer may be convinced enough to make the transition into making a more positive commitment.

Chapter 3:
Be Clear On What You Are Promoting

Synopsis

Getting noticed on the online business arena is only possible if viewers are clear on what they are viewing. Put up ambiguous posting will not help to ensure the target audience nor will it ensure a successful presence on the internet.

Some Tips

Here are some points to consider in ensuring the posting is clear and understood:

- Deciding and designing the material to be posted must follow one theme. When the material posted does not correspond with promotional tone then it can be rather confusing. Therefore the theme should be decided even before the actual designing of the posting is started.

- Understanding what the desired end goal is, contributes to the actual tools and formats that will eventually be utilized. When the goal is clearly identified, then the best suited tools available for internet marketing can be identified for its corresponding contributions.

- Besides the posting content it is also important to provide information on the actual supporting freebies, promotional gimmicks, possible back links, and any other content that would function as an advantage to the viewer visiting the site.

- The posting should also be very clear in the actual visual presentation style so that the viewer will immediately be able to identify with the content without having to resort to various clicks and long winded reading material.

Besides doing all the above using the right platform to get the posting to the target audience is also something that should be given serious consideration.

Newsletter promotion, blog digest, using the social media network, websites, and other forms of making things personal will all help to gain the attention of the target audience effectively.

The promotional plan and promotional strategies should comfortably merge into the same theme. This should in turn have the overall focus of the main achievement being sought.

Chapter 4:
Plan How To Communicate With Others To Convey Professionalism

Synopsis

There are several different aspects that are usually addressed in the quest to stay professionally based with online dealings. The individual has the advantage if professionalism is extended and perceived to exist.

Communication

Perhaps the first area that professionalism should ideally cover is the area of etiquette. The universally accepted common elements would include having the semblance of being polite, being able to address each situation with a level of sincerity, working towards creating satisfies customers and many more.

Taking the time and effort to consider the subscriber list or group as a whole and addressing them as if each one was an individual concern and special would allow the positive basis of the relationship to be built.

Making a positive impact is also another way of portraying professionalism. When the other party is assured that the concerns will be addressed and then ensuring the follow up procedures are followed will create the level of professionalism that few can refute.

Using email addresses that are appropriate and professional sounding is also necessary if one want to be taken seriously in the business arena. Simple but often overlooked is the need to ensure all content is accurately written and factual.

Using a suitable descriptive subject line is also a way to showing professionalism and avoids being identified or classified as spammers who also have casual addressing choices. Being specific, clear, reasonable and to the point is also showing professionalism

as most people do not have the time or inclination to entertain unsolicited interruptions.

The items included in the signature should be of a professional design and content. Unnecessary information should not be included as it would not be deemed necessary.

Ensure all communications is done professionally and with only information sought exchanged. Keep all exchanges short, accurate and to the point.

Chapter 5:
Learn How To Participate With The Community

Synopsis

Using twitter to enhance presence and positioning within the social platform is one of the reasons it was become a much sought after tool. This tool allows the desired traffic to be directed to the site through the twitter exchanges which act indirectly as a good advertising tool.

Check In

The following are some of the recommendations that should be utilized in the quest to participate effectively:

- Making use of the hashtag symbol (#) followed be the name of abbreviation will allow for the sharing of posts between the viewers of a certain group and also follow the twitters connected to the same or similar hashtags. This particular norm has managed to successfully and effectively create the twitter chat that is both exciting and informative.

- For the more experienced twitter dabblers using the twitter chat tool while ensuring the twitter station is well tuned to filter out all unnecessary and annoying noises is important. As there is often a lot of static and other background noises the actual quality of the exchange is more often than not compromised thus the need to intentionally focus on this elimination.

- Upon identification of the hashtag for the desired community or group and the corresponding twitter char tool that is most workable, logging in should be the next step taken. Sometimes timing and dates do play a role, as the particular group chat may only be scheduled to fit a preordained pattern. Also remembering to include the hashtags in one's own tweets is important so that the comments and question posted can be

viewed by other too. In this medium it is also possible to include and also popular to see the expertise of a moderator helping to guide the elements of the discussion to ensure all stay focused on the subject at hand and also some sort of decorum is adhered to.

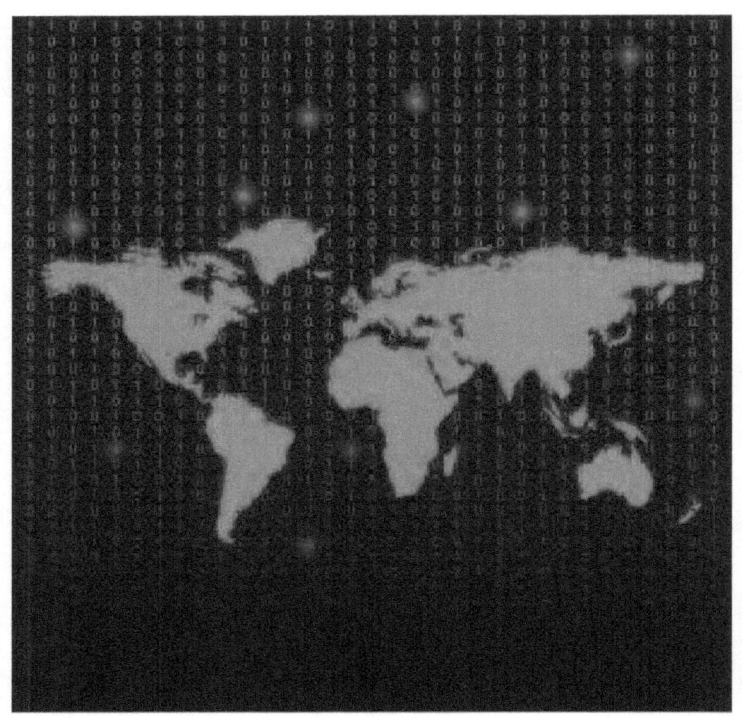

Chapter 6:
Learn How To Make The Most Of Your Account And Profile

Synopsis

There are several effective ways to maximize the use of the twitter tool to enhance the account and profile of a site. The more exposure the site is able to attract the better the prospects of increased revenue earned.

Good Tips

The following are just some recommendations on how to go about achieving this ideal scenario:

- Perhaps the foremost point to make would be to effectively use the twitter tool to find and add newer contacts to an already existing list. The literal concept here is follow and be followed. Using emails as another follow up tool will encourage the viewer to pursue the initial contact.

- Letting the viewing audience know that there is a twitter page where your antics can be followed is part of the social networking engine. Using the other tools on the social networking platform to announce this is quite effective.

- Adding the twitter information to the email signature is also another way to allow and encourage viewers to follow the postings.

- Blogging about the twitter page being featured is also encouraged. Reminding all viewers of the regular intervals of posting through the blogging tool will create the excitement to encourage them to keep tabs on the latest information being dispensed.

- The twitter widget is also another additional beneficial element to make use of as this allows the other viewers to be aware of the frequency of the twitting exercise. The twitter widget should be added to the site of blog.

- Listing on the twitter directories is another way to explore the possibilities of getting noticed. These directories are very effective in getting the site noticed by those seeking similar information.

- Ensuring the twitter page is attractive and attention grabbing will create the interest in wanting to follow the page. Use eye catching background and color schemes, avatars and bio information.

Chapter 7:
Avoid Over Promoting

Synopsis

Over promoting is a very dangerous category to fall into as this may eventually cause the viewing audience to turn elsewhere for the information they seek thus severely damaging the twitter page's chances of making a success of whatever is being featured. Therefore it is necessary to check that this negative element does not appear and cause the damaging effects.

Be Cautious

Twitters have a "language" of their own and understanding and using it is both necessary and beneficial if the individual hosting a twitter site wants to be taken seriously in this arena.

There is a need to ensure the various new terms used as posting material which does not adhere to this will eventually get the site discredited or ignored. Choosing an unsuitable name is also to be avoided as this will cause the professionalism element to be severely discredited and not taken seriously.

Getting into a bragging mode with the intention of promoting something is a thinly disguised attempt to get noticed. When done often enough it will cause the exact opposite effects instead, as those originally viewing the site will end up being exasperated and bored.

Bad choice of timing is also another element to avoid as it may seem that the tweets are being run too frequently and even if the viewing was missed initially.

The unsolicited frequency of the tweeting exercise will eventually cause annoyance as viewers may no longer be interested in the same information being posted.

More often than not this self promoting material can get redundant even if what is being promoted is useful and relevant in the host's perspective.

Repetitive information will become stale. Sometimes when there is too much promoting done, the basic need to address certain issues are overlooked or ignored. This will frustrate the participating viewer as the concerns fail to be addressed effectively.

Chapter 8:
Follow And Use Relevant Tweets

Synopsis

In order to gain beneficial leverage in the online business platform various advantages elements should be sourced and utilized as often as possible. Following and using relevant tweets does have its benefits and it should be worth taking the time and explore this further. Below are some of the reasons why following and using relevant tweets can be useful and beneficial:

Be Relevant

Making use of the hashtags will allow the relevant searches to be more efficient and convenient. It increases the chances of the tweets being viewed by those interested in the particular area being featured. However using multiple hashtags should be avoided as it will only be categorized as spam.

Using twitter to check what the competitors are doing in terms of new launches, promotions, products, services and a variety of other progressive exercises is definitely a wise move to make. This information will help to enhance one's own endeavors and bring about more compatible percentages of increased success.

Tweets should also be carefully analyzed for its popularity and responsive presence. Tweaking the information posted or ideas exchanged in order o attract attention is necessary in order to stay relevant.

In order to do this one must first understand the abbreviations commonly used by the twitting participants. This is the only way one will be able to follow and understand the contents of the tweet.

Wrapping Up

And finally...Keeping track of the hottest and most relevant topics being discussed or feature by twitter participants is important in the quest to stay informed of the market sentiments. This is most important when there are business projections and planning to be explored. Understanding the top trends or interest of the viewing participants will give the individual an idea of what will work and what wont for that particular period in time.

www.ingramcontent.com/pod-product-compliance
Lightning Source LLC
Chambersburg PA
CBHW030559220526
45463CB00007B/3120